D1108175

ZAKISMS™:
LIFE, SIMPLY STATED

by Dr. Zak El-Ramly

Printed in the United States of America
First Printing, 2015
ISBN: 978-0-9862978-0-9
MATTAIN PUBLISHING, LLC, Manal El-Ramly
2416 Trenton Woods Way, Raleigh, NC 27607

www.zakisms.com

ACKNOWLEDGEMENT:

I would like to thank my wife, Salwa, not only for her ability to love me, but also for understanding me, encouraging me, and, most of all, challenging me. She often forces me to practice what I say or observe, so literally, to act on my own quotes.

I would like to also thank my daughter, Manal, without her this book would not have been written, nor would many of the quotes that are in the book exist. Not only did she enjoy my Zakisms (and we are disputing whether she named them Zakisms) but she also showed me that there is potential readership of the quotes, by sharing them with a group of her friends.

I don't like long list of acknowledgements, but in my case the acknowledgements are clear and due, I would like to thank my large family — and my smaller immediate family. They are the ones that give me my life experiences. In that sense, I also have to thank all my friends, colleagues and co-workers and anyone that have come in touch for any duration of time. They all have contributed to my limited understanding of life, its contradictions and the need for eternal compromise.

In the end, I would like to acknowledge and assert that: no one can live by themselves; no one can have it all; no one can always have it his/her way, and the more we are able to compromise, the more there is to share.

DEDICATION:

To my wife, on our 50th anniversary.

Thanks for sharing all these years.

— Zak

"*I started to write my thoughts in short sentences to force myself to focus, reflect, articulate, validate, and generalize my observations about life. I have discovered a major side benefit to my quotes; I am now disciplined to continually review my actions to avoid behaving illogically, irresponsibly, or unethically.*"

Zal

TABLE OF CONTENTS

Dear Reader,

I would like to share with you my collection, *Zakisms: Life, Simply Stated*, which represents the insight I have gained through my personal, social and professional life. I have specifically focused on principles that I have managed to articulate and express in one-liners or a short paragraph — I used to call them quotes.

I like to capture other people's quotes that rhyme with my views on life. Often when I read quotes, either others or mine, I feel the need to elaborate on them and extract more insight. You will see other people's quotes and my thoughts scattered within this book.

I know that many of us learn the same life lessons; the difficulty is recognizing the applicability of our experiences to others and taking the time to express them in words. This book is the articulation of such lessons, as in the last few years I have recognized the added value of verbalizing my insights to make them useable and possibly transferable. I typically write my quotes for my own use first, to debate them in my own mind, and share them only after validating them.

I hope that my Zakisms highlight the ironic nature of life and the eternal need for compromise.

I would love to hear back from you at zak@zakisms.com if any of my quotes strike a positive or negative note with you. I hope my Zakisms provide you with some benefits from my own experience of life. Life has been very good to me and I hope it was and will continue to be the same to you.

Zak

LIFE LESSONS

I was raised in a large and sophisticated family, and as such I had many experiences and observations about life and human interaction imparted on me starting at a very early age. When I started reading quotes others had written, I realized that my observations about life were equally insightful and useful. This first chapter presents my general life lessons and favorite quotes that equally reflect how I think of life.

"It is what it is. It is not what you think it is, not what you hope it would have been, and not what it is supposed to be. Examine it, understand it, deal with the way it is, and stop complaining about it."

Zak

"We attach our own values and attributes to things without carefully measuring the outcome (wishful thinking). We decide what to spend on, what to borrow for, what to give away, what to gift and how charitable we want to be. The problem is that we blame the wrong outcomes on our luck, bad timing or lack of cooperation from God. We credit all positive outcomes to our own smarts."

"You are where you are today because you've chosen to be there."

— Harry Browne

By your actions or choices, whether consciously or subconsciously.

"Going through life is like driving in the city streets — mostly cruising, a bit of acceleration, lots of braking, some stopping, and the odd stall. At the end, it is the average speed that counts."

Zal

Do not change lanes or direction like the maniac who causes accidents or drive like the slowpoke, who is afraid of accidents and strangles traffic. Make sure your engine is tuned up so you do not stall. And remember, failing to stop at a stop sign — breaking the rules — could slow you down further if you get a ticket.

"It is better to be lost trying to get to where you want to go than it is to know where you are but confused about where you want to go."

A clear set of objectives leads you; staying with the status quo will sooner or later stall you.

"Courage is doing what you're afraid to do. There can be no courage unless you're scared."

— Eddie Rickenbacker

"To conquer self, you must first know and understand self. Do not be afraid to explore and test your ideas, emotions and fears."

Zak

"If you do not conquer self, you will be conquered by self."

— Napoleon Hill

"The first and best victory is to conquer self."

— Plato

"Always show your best; think positively, cheerfully, compassionately, and honestly."

Zal

"What's going on in the inside shows on the outside."

— Earl Nightingale

"Life is driven by the efforts and initiatives of a very few of us; if you spot a doer or an innovator, offer help and encouragement, and do not stand in the way. You will be doing yourself a favor."

Zak

"He that walketh with wise men shall be wise."

— Bible, Proverbs 13:20

"Be careful with being too satisfied with your level of effort and success; this could signal the beginning of your demise. Satisfaction with one's own efforts breeds complacency."

"Change before you have to."

— Jack Welch

"Success breeds complacency, complacency breeds failure. Only the paranoid survive."

— Andy Grove

"Do not make decisions in times of emotional extremes, whether exuberance or frustration. Good decisions are made by calmer minds."

Zak

"Action without thinking is the cause of every failure."

— Peter Dreckur

*"When we lack the humility to accept defeat
we compound our losses."*

"No matter how much we have, our resources are finite — material resources, emotional energy and mental capacity. We should not waste our money on extravagant or unneeded items. We should not waste our emotions on unworthy characters or tangential issues. We should not waste our minds engaging in trivia or non-productive discussions."

Zak

"The successful person has the habit of doing the things failures don't like to do. They don't like doing them either necessarily. But their disliking is subordinated to the strength of their purpose."

— E.M. Gray

"Many of us refuse to be happy, simply because we do not believe we are worthy of being happy. Be proud of yourself, be happy; irrespective of whether you think you deserve it or not."

Zal

"Happiness depends upon ourselves."

— Aristotle

PRINCIPLES I LIVE BY

I believe that our emotions and biases interfere with our ability to use sound judgment in areas where right and wrong are blurred. This chapter provides some of what I consider to be the simplest guiding principles of life.

"Giving a rose every other day beats the promise of a rose garden."

Zak

"Never leave that till tomorrow which you can do today."

— Benjamin Franklin

"Truth is what I can always remember, what I can explain again and again and what will surface under examination. It uses up a lot of smarts to maintain a consistent lie; I would rather save mine for productive uses."

Zal

"Accept everything about yourself — I mean everything. You are you, and that is the beginning and the end — no apologies, no regrets."

— Clark Moustakas

The main challenge is knowing who and what you really are to accept yourself with credibility.

"Salvation starts with self-recognition. Improvement starts with self-determination."

Zak

"When we direct our thoughts properly, we can control our emotions."

— W. Clement Stone

"It is your choice: over-value yourself and have others bring you down to earth, or be modest and humble and let them elevate you to your real value."

Zal

"What cannot be explained in simple language is probably not yet well understood."

Maybe we have discovered the symptoms and circumstances, but have not found the real cause or reason yet.

"Making the simple complicated is commonplace; making the complicated simple, awesomely simple, that's creative."

— Charles Mingus

"In good times it is easier to prosper and rise. It is the hard times that differentiate us, expose our qualities and test our endurance."

"Any experience can be transformed into something of value."

— Vash Young

At the very least, you know what you should not do and/or what will not work.

"Those who you will get today will try to get you sooner or later; you are better off doing somebody a favor in the hope it will be returned in the future. In simple language, fill your life bank accounts with good deeds, not with anxious enemies."

Zal

"The ability to discipline yourself to delay gratification in the short term in order to enjoy greater rewards in the long term is the indispensable prerequisite for success."

— Brian Tracy

Think of this next time you are in a meeting and have the urge to say something only to show how smart you are.

"Never leave for tomorrow what you can do today. The simplest reason is that, in this volatile world we live in, we don't know what tomorrow will bring."

Zal

"Opportunity is missed by most people because it is dressed in overalls and feels like work."

— Thomas A. Edison

"Given that he/she who provides the solution inherits the problem, before volunteering a solution, make sure that your contribution is requested, your judgment will be appreciated, and your efforts will be rewarded. Reward need not be financial or immediate, but you must see value. Otherwise you are running interference, wasting time and/or unnecessarily assuming liabilities."

Zak

"Winners are those people who make a habit of doing the things losers are uncomfortable doing."

— Ed Foreman

"If you are given clear instruction you should do your best to follow it, but if you are given any leeway it becomes your responsibility to focus that leeway on optimizing your outcome."

"When you have a number of disagreeable duties to perform, always do the most disagreeable first."

— Josiah Quincy

"In my eventful life I have insulted, offended or threatened more people unintentionally than intentionally. Humans are more fragile and sensitive than most of us recognize and need their egos brushed constantly, despite the façade we all like to put up to the contrary."

As I keep on getting older, I try to learn and increase my sensitivity; still, I keep on underestimating the emotional fragility of human beings.

"To be successful you have to be selfish, or else you never achieve. And once you get to your highest level, then you have to be unselfish. Stay reachable. Stay in touch. Don't isolate."

— Michael Jordan

"Sometimes the cost of being kind pales in comparison to the value to others; it is our selfishness, indifference or false pride that stops us from performing acts of kindness."

Zal

"No act of kindness, no matter how small, is ever wasted."

— Aesop

WE ARE
ONLY HUMAN

As humans we are simultaneously weak, strong and vulnerable. But acknowledging our strengths, weaknesses and vulnerabilities can safeguard us. In the following chapter, I offer some of the most obvious observations that we may choose to ignore, deny or hide for our own comfort.

Zal

"We mix reasons and excuses. A good excuse does not make for a good reason. If we have a good reason, we do not need an excuse."

Zak

"Never accept the proposition that just because a solution satisfies a problem, that it must be the only solution."

— Raymond E. Feist

Or conversely, that if you have a good idea, you can make it a solution to a non-existing problem.

"Often, the evidence and self-incriminations needed for proof will come voluntarily from the person under suspicion."

Because we typically analyze things from a self-centered or twisted perspective. So listen and ask before accusing; you may get your evidence easier.

"One needs to be slow to form conviction, but once formed, they must be defended against the heaviest odds."

— Mohandas Gandhi

"Foolishness is to ignore the probability and consequences of failure. Cowardice is to make the fear of failure stop us from trying."

Zak

The only thing that stops us from getting our dreams is the fear of failure.

"Do what you fear most and you control fear."

— Tom Hopkins

"Sometimes we try to knock down what is otherwise a very viable argument because we fear a conclusion it might lead to."

"If you think you can handle your conflict, potential conflict or the appearance of conflict on your own, you are already conflicted. If you can justify not being honorable, you are already being dishonorable. If you think you can hide your dirt, you are already tainted. If you only tell white lies, you are still a liar."

Because of our natural bias, self-centered, and self-righteous attitude and our stupid ego, using ourselves to judge or justify our own questionable actions is a slippery slope.

"If you're never scared or embarrassed or hurt, it means you never take any chances."

— Julia Sorel

"You cannot choose when to be virtuous. You are, or you are not."

Zal

"Confidence .... thrives only on honesty, on honor, on the sacredness of obligations, on faithful protection and on unselfish performance. Without them, it cannot live."

— Franklin D. Roosevelt

"What makes thinking hard is not the intensity or complexity of the subject or the issue, it is the emotions attached to it."

Zak

"Anyone can become angry — that is easy. But to be angry with the right person, to the right degree, at the right time, for the right purpose, and in the right way — that is not easy."

— Aristotle

"Unnecessary explanation or justification for one's action exposes the risk of the explanation being the reason for rejecting the action when the action itself was not in question."

We usually provide explanations and excuses because of our continuous need for approval from others, not because the explanation is expected or required.

"Thus to be independent of public opinion is the first formal condition of achieving anything great."

— G. W. F. Hegel

"Feedback is only criticism when the recipient takes it that way."

Zal

We convert feedback to criticism when we are unable to explain ourselves, unwilling to look into the mirror, resent the implied need for a change or are unable to trust the intent of the sender. Interestingly, we typically blame the sender for something or another rather than dealing with the essence or content of the message.

"Honest criticism is hard to take, particularly from a relative, a friend, an acquaintance or a stranger."

— Franklin P. Jones

"We all like to project composure, logic and fairness, even when we are at the edge, illogical and biased."

In the process, we trick ourselves as much as we hope to trick others.

"Be like a duck. Calm on the surface, but always paddling like the dickens underneath."

— Michael Caine

"Our self-focus often hampers our ability to understand the emotions of others and causes us to misinterpret their reactions: we think they are angry when they are disappointed; we find them offensive when they are insecure; we may blame them for indifference when they are really afraid or deem them irresponsible when they are merely incompetent. Our lack of empathy aggravates their ills."

This is a very hard lesson to learn because we take things personally and want to get even before understanding where the others are coming from or why they act the way they do. We are suspicious by nature.

"We are masters at hiding our true feelings and weaknesses. The problem is that we may also hide our feelings from ourselves, delaying our ability to confront them and denying ourselves the potential support and understanding of others."

"Whatever anybody says or does, assume positive intent .... When you assume negative intent, you're angry."

— Indra Nooyi

Remember that sometimes what you believe you see is not really what is going on; the other party may be failing to communicate, hiding true feelings, or you yourself may be tainted by your current mood and bias.

"It is much easier and more graceful to admit you are wrong than to force others to prove it to you."

Zak

"I am now sure globalization works. We globalized trade, travel and the use of the internet. We also globalized porn, terrorism and economic crises. I am not sure globalization worked the way we wanted it to work."

"Be careful what you wish for. You just might receive it."

— Old proverb – disputed origin

THE COMPLEXITIES OF LIVING

Many situations are multi-faceted and often ironic, making life feel complex. In this chapter, I try to highlight some of these ironies to facilitate understanding of some of the complexities of life.

"A most difficult aspect of learning is un-learning what has already been learned."

Zak

So your mind can accept the new observations and replace the dated ones.

"There is only one thing more painful than learning from experience and that is not learning from experience."

— Archibald McLeish

"The facts are seldom confusing. What is confusing is finding the facts (or what constitutes a fact), accepting the facts and dealing with the facts."

"The brighter you are, the more you have to learn."

— Don Herold

"Unnecessary compliments or flattery may have
some soothing effects on a recipient, but the soothing
value to a recipient must be weighed against the cost
for a giver of appearing manipulative, intellectually
dishonest or lacking seriousness or credibility."

Zak

"To be persuasive we must be believable; to be
believable we must be credible; to be credible we must
be truthful."

— Edward R. Murrow

"Never take the inability to express or articulate as an indication of a lack of ability to understand or appreciate."

"The closer we are to achieving our goals or dreams, the more obsessed we can become with them."

At that point, the thrill of making "it" is the reward, not the original object of the goal (material or otherwise).

"Think of yourself as on the threshold of unparalleled success. A whole clear, glorious life lies before you. Achieve! Achieve!"

— Andrew Carnegie

"Often it is not an event that puts us in a certain mood; we have already decided what mood we want to be in, and we are only looking for a reason to justify our feeling."

Zal

"One's ships come in over a calm sea."

— Florence Scovill Shinn

"We can do a lot if we really want to. The real problem is that we often do not have the necessary drive or don't believe we deserve to have what we want."

Zak

"Everything's in the mind. That's where it all starts. Knowing what you want is the first step toward getting it."

— Mae West

"You, too, can determine what you want. You can decide on your major objectives, targets, aims and destination."

— W. Clement Stone

"We mostly have a choice in actions we initiate, but seldom have control over the reaction of others to our actions."

Zal

Only do those things which you can deal with or accept the results of.

"The wise man avoids evil by anticipating it."

— Unknown

"When we start blaming others for our shortcomings, we are setting the stage for our own failures."

Zak

"He is free ... who knows how to keep in his own hand the power to decide."

— Salvador De Madariaga

"As we get older and our value system and judgment evolves, we rewrite our memories in the hopes of reducing our guilt or shame."

"One's dignity may be assaulted, vandalized and cruelly mocked, but cannot be taken away unless it is surrendered."

— Michael J. Fox

"Three tests to gauge the prudence of our actions: our willingness to have what we do exposed; the degree of our ability to manage the outcome; and our capacity to accept the results."

Remember, the truth always surfaces; we have less control than we think, and no risk results in no reward.

"Nothing can stop the man with the right mental attitude from achieving his goal: Nothing on earth can help the man with the wrong mental attitude."

— Thomas Jefferson

"When people start to argue the point by providing reasons or excuses, they have already accepted the premise or observation."

Zal

LIFE, THE ETERNAL COMPROMISE

Right and wrong, fair and unfair, and good and bad are never measured equally among humans. To live harmoniously requires continual judgment depending on the circumstances we are in, hence the need for eternal compromise. In this chapter, I offer some examples of the essence of life.

Zal

"The irony in life and business is that they are filled with contradictions. One needs to care enough to win, but not be troubled if one loses. Deal with credibility and establish trust, but not depend on that credibility or trust. Be generous in giving, but expect frugality in receiving."

Zak

"If you don't like something, change it. If you can't change it, change your attitude. Don't complain."

— Maya Angelou

"Our prerogatives come with their own costs and liabilities."

"If you want the rainbow, you've got to put up with the rain."

— Jimmy Durante

"There is no meaning to life without death, no feeling of happiness if we have not experienced sadness, no richness if there is no poorness, no up without down, and nothing is full unless it was once empty."

Zak

There is some good, even in the very bad.

"Those who do not know how to weep with their whole heart don't know how to laugh either."

— Golda Meir

"Sometimes we are so obsessed with proving our observations, conclusions or predictions right, we miss or ignore the cost of proving them, or even that we would be better off wrong."

"It's always worthwhile to make others aware of their worth."

— Malcolm Forbes

"The value of money is latent; until you spend your money, you have not truly earned or benefitted from it yet."

"Everything you want in life has a price connected to it. There's a price to pay if you want to make things better, a price to pay just for leaving things as they are; a price for everything."

— Harry Browne

"If we are fortunate enough to be spared the hard times, we should gracefully preserve, appreciate and share our good fortune."

"The meeting of preparation with opportunity generates the offspring we call luck."

— Anthony Robbin

"Sometimes our reason or excuse is worse than the offence itself. It is better to not have one and be truly sorry than to further incriminate yourself."

Zak

"The man who makes no mistakes does not usually make anything."

— William Connor Magee

"Just think about it — you can always find a reason to be in a good mood, and you can also find more reasons to be in a bad mood. The track you take will always produce the results thought."

Zol

"The best things in life have little to do with money or success. They are based on heart, compassion and allowing others to express their passions."

— Declan Dunn

"It is ironic that those who demand respect have difficulty respecting, those who ask for love do not know it starts by giving it, and those who think they are righteous always doubt the morality or sincerity of others."

Zak

"When nobody around you measures up, it's time to check your yardstick."

— Bill Lemly

"The most devastating fights are with those who are close or dear to us, not only because we lose or hurt them, but also because they know where, when and how to get us."

Zal

"Nurture great thoughts for you cannot go higher than your thoughts."

— Benjamin Disraeli

"Shit happens, and often we have no hand in it. When it does, we are confronted with choices: do nothing and allow it to stink, cover it up to hopefully reduce the smell, or clean up and start fresh again."

Zak

"Life is very ironic — it takes a very long time to build, but it is very easy and fast to destroy; this applies to structures and equipment, humans and other living things, wealth, career and reputation."

Zal

"A man masters nature not by force but by understanding."

— Jacob Bronowski

Success breeds success.

Failure breeds experience.

Experience breeds success.

ABOUT THE AUTHOR

Dr. Zak El-Ramly (Zak) is founder of the ZE family of companies (www.ze.com). The first member of the family, ZE PowerGroup Inc. was established in 1995. ZE is now a group of interrelated, globally positioned organizations that provide enterprise-level software solutions, consulting and support services and design engineering for large and small-scale organizations in many industries.

ZE is the developer of the award-winning enterprise data management software solution, ZEMA, with offices and clients across the globe. ZE has satellite offices in Vancouver, Raleigh, Houston, New York, Calgary, Madrid, and Maastricht. Service operations are based in Vancouver, the UK and Singapore.

Zak's leadership extends to a diverse group of professionals from all over the world, further exposing him to professional and multicultural diversity. His vision and ambition drive the success the ZE family of companies enjoys today.

A significant portion of Zak's business experience came from working for BC Hydro, where Zak constantly pushed the organization into cutting terrain. His experience in leadership at BC Hydro has been in conservation, planning, and business management in regulated and deregulated environments. Zak has acted as an expert witness in many regulatory forums.

Zak was born and raised in Port-Said, Egypt. Zak has been happily married since 1965 to his loving and supportive wife, Salwa, who is a driver behind Zak's success. Their four children, Aiman, Waleed, Manal and Nader have risen to carry key management roles at ZE, and with their diverse skill sets, are instrumental in the success of ZE. He is blessed with 10 grandchildren, who add further fulfillment, challenge and stimulation to his life.

Dr. El-Ramly has a PhD in Aeronautical Engineering from Carleton University and a masters and bachelors in Mechanical Engineering. Zak is a Canadian Professional Engineer.

Extracting observations about life in simple quotes is an intellectual stimulating and inspirational activity for Zak. We hope his quotes are equally reflective and inspirational to you.

CPSIA information can be obtained at www.ICGtesting.com
Printed in the USA
LVIW01n1507111115
461962LV00004BA/5

* 9 7 8 0 9 8 6 2 9 7 8 0 9 *